Don't Call Me A Poet

Meader

Forward:

"Speak like your breaths are numbered

and sing like you can't count."

Thank you to everyone who has supported me in my writing and in life. To my muses and to all those I have cared for; you continue to inspire me to this day. I have written this collection over 30 years of life and am proud to have the opportunity and means to be able to publish it. I welcome any and all reactions, and hope you find this to be an enjoyable experience.
Thank you, good reader.

Copyright © 2020 Meader
All rights reserved.

Star Crossed

You shine: A star refusing to be drowned out by the city lights when deep inside a passion burns and bursts upon the canvas overhead a welcome savior to mine tired eyes.

I pine; for night cannot arrive with too much haste. The light the sun provides strikes not upon the place inside my chest where darkness dances in your graceful glow your very nature springs, imbibing in your waters I'm alive but falter, why would such a life be lived alone? Admired, sure, but fire in a weightless vortex shatters while the same upon a wick becomes a wish - everlasting.

Through time I travelled tearing 'cross the cosmos for the lifespan of a soul and when at last your source was reached your shine had all been stripped, your burning passion ceased and null. I searched the empty sea of space for who had called my name cross time, and all the while failed to see the light was of itself your being.

Crushed

Your mind it functions differently.

It's like there's logic but it's clogged with creativity, cogs move independently yet somehow in insanity there's clarity - a masterpiece.

Keeping time so perfectly behind the scenes, but those who read the face alone are missing beauty hid beneath.

Expectations overturned, imbued with ingenuity; impervious to paradigms a lonely life to lead but freedom's never free.

I've been struck a thousand times by beauty in the carnate sense, like lightning passing head to toe then flowing on to somewhere else; and though the electricity is felt it seems to linger overwhelming in my head it's so impeding yet it feels like home.

I've only known you for a month. And yet you just keep popping up inside my thoughts and when we talk there's such a rush like holy fuck there's someone else who gets my humor, thinks in tongues, it's such a rarity for me, guess you could say I have a crush - to say the least.

Muse

You could keep me waiting

I'd be patient as I'm sated

By your steel blue staring

Sneaking glances; stealing air

Deprive my lungs - derive my longing

You're the chorus to the songs that once felt hollow in their place is now the beating of a heart

And yes, I know that this is forward in exaggerated form but only when a muse lends beauty can the purest art be born.

You're Too Hard On Yourself

To save yourself it's best to start by saving someone else. It may feel you're diving deeper but remember that your world is upside down. See yourself honestly, free that selfish modesty, you're not meant for mediocrity; your mind's a mesmerizing moment making music silently. It's times like these that tear our eyes; those who feel the darkest often have the brightest shine. Pray for kindness in the lives of liars, thieves, the vilified. Allow your heart release and really read the roughest rhyming righteous writings you once threw beneath. And this time keep them.

Brainstorm

I see a scene, the sea I've seen,
it seems to me the scenery;
It screams.
I cease to breathe,
yet beastly breezes bleed the trees of beaks and bees of every breed.
Secretly I sheathe my seething
Jealousy like seeds they're seated
Deepening; their need to feed is
Subtly a reason for the seasons to give way to a release.

Take A Bow

Four equestrians of misery
The quest began in mystery
By questioning the ministry
The quenching of the thirsty trees
Begins with restless Nurseries merciless is merchantry, uncertainty is seemingly feeding the freedom that they seek
Bursting at the seams the seeds they seep into the scenery, speaking so uneasily whilst feasting, wilting wildebeest, what will they see? Their wills deplete, and still their silver tongues spew seething secrets out of jealousy.
Melt with me, selfishly we'll meld to be a memory.
We're meant to be,
mentally unmitigated motivation making mountains sink beneath.
Simply breathe,
centuries untold unfold as sailors sing from wretched deeps, through clenched teeth, the blessed preach while those who lose the most get told to roll on over back to sleep; keep the peace.
The reaper's sweetest tragedy is sneaking silence into minds alive with tantalizing dreams,
seize the day and free the beat, when praying try to keep receipts, never lay where others eat.
Let the music wash you clean, let workers win and sinners weep.
Synergy is paramount to why the meek are given ground.
Scream aloud, feed the crowded masses with your sickest sounds.
Never lose the mood that muses will allow, write it down.
Reject the crown until you've found yourself and then remember how you came about.
Save your doubt for when your voice picks choices other face, then think it out.
And when it's time for stepping down, turn around to see the life you led and if you'd like to,
take a bow.

Return To Sender

Step into the madness
Ripped apart by sadness
Letters being ravaged
Twisted by the savage

Longing

My first crush,
My first love,
That first rush from the first puff
The last dance,
An everlasting trance
My last chance at romance
There's a lot of things in life I chase to try to make the feelings play again
but I'd replace them all if it would make you stay;
I miss your face.

Gold Dust

You left me all alone when you turned into a phone,
and the phone became a stone,
and the stone could dull the senses, turn the silence into gold.
This grew old, as feelings do, maybe that's why seeing you
now terrifies me in the place where my red heart turned to blue.
At long last losing all the blackness that had found its way in through
the throbbing hole you left when loving hands
crept through my back into my chest
and tried to kill the golden goose who shone with hues that you could use.
Why still does my heart beat in tune with your impatient feet,
it's used to being treated like a fool,
but truth be told it's been defeated.
Ruthless to the core must be the one whose craft is shattered dreams.

On Trust

I'm left confounded by the creatures
crawling from the sutures
that are keeping peeping toms from spying secrets
hidden deep beneath the surface of the sheets that wrap our bones
and soul
yet those who do deserve the chance
to delve into your world are turned away at the gate,
or met with venom and hate,
as slick tongues slip through thick shells and raise hell.

Human Flesh

I'm like a hungry animal
A feeding cannibal
Fiendishly feasting on the flesh of lesser minds
as men are fleeing, fighting for their lives
but foolish lies and feeble rhymes
have flushed their hopes of keeping up with me to flight,
alas a lightning bolt has locked the locker door
that keeps my lunch alive for moments longer
lingering laughter lines the halls and soils laundry.
Stall all you like,
inevitability is ripe and ready to be plucked like harp strings at night,
those sharp stings are bites
being taken from your fake and fragile ego,
I'm the hero here.
Heroic intentions,
my methods demented,
You see demonic possession,
I see divine intervention.

Smolder

The quiet unrest of the night
A riot protesting for rights
A choir song sung out of sight
A fire sunk deep down inside
In the oceans through which you see
Passion boils waters beneath
I sink to the bottom; I'm free
Find pockets of air; I can breathe

When Today Becomes Yesterday

Every tick of the clock,
Every beat of your heart,
Every second that's gone,
Every thought that's been lost
Has left you feeling so stuck
Like maybe you're not enough
Yeah, learning lessons is tough
But don't give up on your love

To You, Love

It's hard to believe that after all of this time I still find your eyes divine.
Your kind words and bright mind,
making my heart rise up, sublime creating clouds that rain down,
I feel alive,
alight with infatuation's curse,
your smile alive inside my head undressed, exposed,
not embarrassed or exploited,
rather free to be myself for the first time in a long while,
and thus this prose in an attempt
to show you how I feel.

Smile

The sun's last rays before escaping from a day's work.
The smell after a rainstorm has swallowed up your whole world.
The star-stained sky as you lie awake and cry.
A priceless diamond stone in the lighting of the moonshine.
Try as I might I can't fight this feeling that even the most beautiful images
are nothing in comparison to you;
And you have no clue.

Restless

Premonitions peak when the shadows smother light
As the ghosts and ghouls all slither forth from deep within our minds.
Separation speaks the sharpest sounds in darkest night
Spewing acrid affirmations that attack us from behind.
Through the useless walls we build,
every demon that we've killed,
every toss and turn and tumble,
every hole we've tried to fill
sneaks and snakes the things that shake
our very frame, we lie awake.
It's these helpless, hopeless moments hiding deep within our sheets
That we must learn to beat if we ever want to sleep
Peacefully.

On The Perversion Of Religion

Exquisitely written, these scriptures to be given to the masses.
Twisted and bitten by the ignorant classes
where the mystery's masked by misdirection toward fact.
The power residing in these letters combined into visions
is mistakenly driving those who require the very guidance
that was intended but has since been amended,
blinding the love anc hiding the spirit we all feel inside
but don't quite know how to let shine
so instead we let pride take the best of us and fry what our ribs hide
until we're all numb to each other.

On Fate

Life ain't a single line, it's a path covered in vines
like the subtle trails of deer through the wooded bars of fear.
Sometimes the path will end, but ahead the next begins
and it's the roads that we create, in between the ones well paved
that reflect our inner soul, our deepest passions and our goals.
Fate may not be some AI drive, a choice-less, sheepy drole,
but rather just a gentle guide, a forking in the road.

Fallen Angel, Hear My Plea

The lighthouse calls I make for you
go unheeded, blindly driving towards the rocky shore,
gathering speed;
committed.
The madness a blur of romantic hope
scarlet waves of satisfaction
assurance, promises;
committed.
And when he's had his fun and moves on
I'll miss you when you're gone,
inside yourself;
committed.

Valentine

She moves through time like the rhythm through a rhyme
and she kicks her feet clean as she steps out to the streets.
Keeps gum in her pocket, a gun in her purse,
and with a smile she can take you on a trip around the Earth.
A razor blade tongue and a diamond cut mind,
the kind of girl to knock you on your back in record time.

Clocks With Wings

I sit here staring at a rusted hammer, the gel-grip handle worn down to cold steel and fraying in every direction, the neck such a dark orange/brown that a single swing of the once well-loved tool would surely send its head to the floor. I stare and consider how useless it is when not being beaten and how such a majestic, powerful tool can lose all value through non-use. And now I'm left wondering: Can you empathize with an inanimate object?

Lost

Her eyes stain the canvas spread out at her feet
with colorless shades keeping time to the beat.
She swore to herself that she'd never break down again
over what could have been, but the ghost still got in.
And now her rocking chair heart has been splintered to bits
by movie screen images that just don't exist.
If she'd pick up the phone and give freedom to truth
the sunshine would dry her eyes right to the root,
but when deep seeded fears of rejection aren't fought
hope turns from a
~~w o u l d b e~~, to
~~c o u l d b e~~, to
n o t.

Sky Angels

Frozen flakes float effortlessly down into chilly clustered crowds.
Feather fragments glimmer and shine as she worryingly furrows her brow.
Deducing the stars must have fallen to Earth as the night sky is darkened as pitch,
She packs them together in a tight, icy ball and steadies her feet in the ditch.
"I'll help you home, lost beauties" she yells towards the canvas displayed up above,
Then she smiles so bright it paints light 'cross the night, releasing the lost glacial dove.

Lullaby

Though there's miles 'tween our beds and all alone in mine I lay,
It's your smile in my head that keeps the loneliness at bay.
As the stars all shine above and the moonlight streaks the skies,
I'm reminded of the lightning bugs that sparkle in your eyes.
So let's release those burdens gained from all our arbitrary trials
And be whisked off into sleep once more, if only for a while.

Hoping For A Happy Ending

Like reading a book with poison laced paper,
you're killing yourself with every turn of the page
and yet you just must know how it ends.

Articulation

Art is what happens when your mind can't think because your heart is screaming too loudly;
Vomit
An artist translates between body and soul;
A transistor
Art is empathetic apathy;
Who cares
An artist creates art;
Antithesis
Art is a perversion of the universal vernacular;
Transcendent of communication
An artist is a daredevil, a coward, a martyr, a savior, a damner, a rebel
Art is the most specific form of generalization;
A sad smile
An artist is someone who, while everyone pretends to sing in harmony, sings silently with their weapon;
A villain
Art is meditated spontaneity;
Muffin
An artist is anyone who has ever felt such a fierce emotion that they **had** to share;
Family
Art is affinity between two complete strangers;
Long lost twins
An artist is someone who can drag you sometimes willingly into your imagination, your dreams, your nightmares, deep within your own mind, your memory, to experience those emotions again;
The monster under your bed
And to those who can do that, I pay my greatest respects, because it's exceedingly onerous.

Princess

I would slay monsters and dragons and trolls,
as I travel the vastest of lands that unfold.
I'd battle through armies collecting their gold
and buy the most powerful sword ever sold
to rescue my maiden from evil and beasts
and waken her gently from deep within sleep.
The maiden I rescue need not be most fair
with beautiful dresses and flowing blonde hair.
She need not have eyes that could rival the stars,
have virgin white skin or be free of all scars.
There's only one thing I'd require be shown;
she's willing to fight by my side 'til we're home

Of a Feather

The saddest sound I've ever heard
was the singing of a lovesick bird
and though this story sounds absurd
it's true, I swear to every word.
I listened to her call for days,
warming with the sun's first rays
and on a single branch she stayed
and cried her song in every shade.
It started out a yellow tune
so full of life, but all too soon
it faded to a deeper red
as longing slipped inside her head.
From there it changed to faded green
and stayed that way for weeks it seemed
until the day that I awoke
to hear the sounds of fading hope;
she whistled out a purple hue,
a color I most surely knew.
As anger made her rhythm crack
her gentle tweeting tinted black
but she refused to self-disdain
so from all noise she did refrain.
For weeks on end I turned and tossed,
my bones made brittle by the frost,
I knew deep down that I had lost
that voice that colored in my thoughts.
Until, one night, I woke from sleep
to those familiar, gentle tweets
and empathetic tears did spew;
her melody had turned to blue.

Camouflage

My mouth is full of clotted blood,
cut by razor shards of love.
The scars I hide within my cheeks
are poking out like feet from sheets.
These words are barbed; a wired fence
and yanked from deep within my chest,
tearing through my vocal chords
and dripping blood upon the floor.
Passing over leather lips,
once fully pulled by fingertips
out from the hollow cave it rips
through bones and flesh, my teeth get chipped
from biting down on steely hooks
and safety scissor dirty looks.
So now I hide from sharpened crooks
behind these old decaying books.

Insomnia

As I shake my head in silence letters tumble from my ears,
pushed out of cognition by a thousand grinding gears.
They splash onto the pages in an aimless mess of ink;
the dripping sounds of water in an empty kitchen sink.
Once muted vagrant cells, I'm now unable to ignore
so I'm forced to make some sense of all these gaudy, vexing spores.
Once they're put in place they quiet down like bashful sheep
and the ringing in my attic quells so I can get some sleep.

Dissension

Spiders' tangled webs are weaved
from silver strands of misbelief.
Like there's a chew toy in my chest,
the place where vultures make their nests,
filthy birds.
So I'll spend my days in dreaming
and my nights in mental breaming
though my molded heart is beating
still my fingertips are bleeding
empty words.

Dyspnea

I dreamt of you all last night.
You were walking away from me for hours, choking on a chain-link leash.
I was never quite sure if you realized you held the lead, not I,
But you kept calling out to me anyway;
your voice gently fading yet your image immaculate.
Your lungs finally gave out after innumerable whispers
so in mercy I attempted to sever the tether.
I have never heard a scream so loud
as that of your freedom.
I awoke exhausted, and ever since,
silence eludes me.

Dietary Supplements

I dine on hope; nutrition value low.
And the taste? You don't even want to know.
But when she looks at me and smiles, when her vision crosses mine,
I am feasting on this tofu square, the spice of love; divine.
And I could live my life on hope alone until I meet my doom,
if you would always be the flavoring to all that I consume.

Restless

Premonitions peak when the shadows smother light
As the ghosts and ghouls all slither forth from deep within our minds.
Separation speaks the sharpest sounds in darkest night
Spewing acrid affirmations that attack us from behind.
Through the useless walls we build,
every demon that we've killed,
every toss and turn and tumble,
every hole we've tried to fill
sneaks and snakes the things that shake
our very frame, we lie awake.
It's these helpless, hopeless moments hiding deep within our sheets
That we must learn to beat if we ever want to sleep
Peacefully.

Nouns (You)

A bracelet scribed 'breathe'
The rose in my cheeks
A promise I keep
The cat at my feet
A bus ticket receipt
Not a song, just the beat
A freeze when I sleep
The reason I weep

Sliced sun through the blinds
An icy incline
Confection divine
Decay in rewind
Smiling eyes
A flutter inside
Laughter through time
The reason I rhyme

Breaking of bones
Text on a phone
A word all alone
The coldest of stones
Hair in a comb
A house not a home
A fade where you shone
Reduced to a poem

Box Shaped Heart

I tie little bits of myself to everything I own,
The odor is sweet to me alone;
I watch as they decay.
I've given the entirety of my heart to people I'll never meet
And imbibe their beauty selfishly;
Such a useless organ anyway.

Nightmare

Cold sweat is cliche, yet my jaw drips.
The silence stirs a thousand lurking pupils in my mind;
they're staring outward grabbing light to shade the shadows darker,
set my mind away from visions crafted back in moments years before my eyes were opened.
Maybe if I sleep again this waking feel will fall away –
maybe…

Hope

With a heart divine as only Love could make it,
even the bittering Sorrow exhales sweetened

www.ingramcontent.com/pod-product-compliance
Lightning Source LLC
Chambersburg PA
CBHW060544030426
42337CB00021B/4432